Editor-in-Chief and Founder:
Lyndon H. LaRouche, Jr.
Editorial Board: *Lyndon H. LaRouche, Jr. , Helga Zepp-LaRouche, Robert Ingraham, Tony Papert, Gerald Rose, Dennis Small, Jeffrey Steinberg, William Wertz*
Co-Editors: *Robert Ingraham, Tony Papert*
Managing Editor: *Nancy Spannaus*
Technology: *Marsha Freeman*
Books: *Katherine Notley*
Ebooks: *Richard Burden*
Graphics: *Alan Yue*
Photos: *Stuart Lewis*
Circulation Manager: *Stanley Ezrol*

INTELLIGENCE DIRECTORS
Counterintelligence: *Jeffrey Steinberg, Michele Steinberg*
Economics: *John Hoefle, Marcia Merry Baker, Paul Gallagher*
History: *Anton Chaitkin*
Ibero-America: *Dennis Small*
Russia and Eastern Europe: *Rachel Douglas*
United States: *Debra Freeman*

INTERNATIONAL BUREAUS
Bogotá: *Miriam Redondo*
Berlin: *Rainer Apel*
Copenhagen: *Tom Gillesberg*
Houston: *Harley Schlanger*
Lima: *Sara Madueño*
Melbourne: *Robert Barwick*
Mexico City: *Gerardo Castilleja Chávez*
New Delhi: *Ramtanu Maitra*
Paris: *Christine Bierre*
Stockholm: *Ulf Sandmark*
United Nations, N.Y.C.: *Leni Rubinstein*
Washington, D.C.: *William Jones*
Wiesbaden: *Göran Haglund*

ON THE WEB
e-mail: eirns@larouchepub.com
www.larouchepub.com
www.executiveintelligencereview.com
www.larouchepub.com/eiw
Webmaster: *John Sigerson*
Assistant Webmaster: *George Hollis*
Editor, Arabic-language edition: *Hussein Askary*

EIR (ISSN 0273-6314) *is published weekly (50 issues), by EIR News Service, Inc., P.O. Box 17390, Washington, D.C. 20041-0390. (703) 777-9451*

European Headquarters: E.I.R. GmbH, Postfach Bahnstrasse 9a, D-65205, Wiesbaden, Germany Tel: 49-611-73650
Homepage: http://www.eirna.com
e-mail: eirna@eirna.com
Director: Georg Neudecker

Montreal, Canada: 514-461-1557

Denmark: EIR - Danmark, Sankt Knuds Vej 11, basement left, DK-1903 Frederiksberg, Denmark. Tel.: +45 35 43 60 40, Fax: +45 35 43 87 57. e-mail: eirdk@hotmail.com.

Mexico City: EIR, Sor Juana Inés de la Cruz 242-2 Col. Agricultura C.P. 11360 Delegación M. Hidalgo, México D.F. Tel. (5525) 5318-2301
eirmexico@gmail.com

Postmaster: Send all address changes to *EIR*, P.O. Box 17390, Washington, D.C. 20041-0390.

Signed articles in *EIR* represent the views of the authors, and not necessarily those of the Editorial Board.

I0413912

Putin's Secret Weapon

EIR Contents

www.larouchepub.com Volume 43, Number 21, May 20, 2016

Cover This Week

Russia's President Vladimir V. Putin

kremlin.ru

I. PUTIN'S SECRET WEAPON

3 EDITORIAL
Sub Specie Aeternitatis: A Moment Out of Time

4 LYNDON LAROUCHE
You've Got to Fill Mankind with Greatness

II. STOP THE WAR: REMOVE OBAMA

10 **In the Face of World War III**
by Dave Christie

16 **A Moment of Truth for America and Her Citizens**
by Jeffrey Steinberg and Robert Ingraham

19 NEW PARTY IN GERMANY
The AfD Party: Old Wine in New Bottles?
by Helga Zepp-LaRouche

III. THE NEW SILK ROAD

22 YEMEN
Readings of EIR World Land-Bridge Report Become National Events

24 **What a Brave and Beautiful New World!**
Mohammed Aref reviews the Arabic translation of *The New Silk Road Becomes the World Land-Bridge* for *Al-Ittihad*, Abu Dhabi, UAE

25 HELGA ZEPP-LAROUCHE
'Looking at the Map of Africa, One Can See That It Lacks Basic Infrastructure'

28 **South Africa's ANC: British Use Regime Change to Stop BRICS**
by David Cherry and Ramasimong Phillip Tsokolibane

EDITORIAL

Sub Specie Aeternitatis: A Moment Out of Time

May 12—Our historians are monumentally incompetent. Things do not happen: Rather, they are made to happen.

But made how? By tricks? By schemes? By the kind of "knowledge" produced by ambition? By calculation?

On May 10, a few of us were privileged beyond all measure to partake in a unique, and indeed an epochal historic encounter with the 93-year-old Lyndon H. La-Rouche, Jr., on a hilltop in Virginia. The influence, and along with it the memory of his presentation there, will long outlive everyone who was present. And yet, even so, LaRouche stated that it was only the first of a series; where this will go in the immediate future can hardly be imagined.

This is a man who has profoundly changed the history of the Twentieth and Twenty-First Centuries,—with completely deliberate intention, but by using nothing but his own highly controversial methods. He has changed the history of these decades using his mind alone, without weapons or budgets. Or whatever weapons or budgets he may have had at any time, he obtained using his unique methods, while he was "understood by very few, and supported by no one," as Einstein said of Johannes Kepler.

How is this possible? Common sense and practicality reject it completely,— yet it has happened. Not only that, but it is happening now. And it was visibly happening on May 10,— for those who were able to see it.

Neither a transcript nor an audio recording could capture anything of the eye-to-eye communication of May 10. That you can only reproduce for yourself, inside yourself.

But we can begin to get at it by stating what it is not. Common-sense thinking separates out goals, methods, ideas, and motivations as four distinct things,— four types. But for LaRouche and for the other heirs of Plato, such as Russia's Vladimir Putin, they are not separate at all: They are all just different views or images of precisely one and the same quality, somewhat as when you view one diamond (and through it the world), through various of its different facets. The true and the only source of the power to change history,— the only source of history,— is the inexhaustible spring of the one single "quality," which was at the center of LaRouche's presentation of May 10.

He began it by saying that he was devoting the remainder of his life to rescuing human creativity. He went on to say that he was in process of making improvements in his movement, that it must rise to a higher standard. History hangs in the balance.

Some of LaRouche's words on that occasion are reported below, but these words are only the palest shadows of what was being communicated.

LYNDON LAROUCHE

You've Got To Fill Mankind With Greatness

May 10—The following are excerpts from an address to associates by Lyndon LaRouche today.

It is the ability to create a new future, to create a development of a future that you had never known before or since. That's your obligation. Don't be practical; don't say, "I'm being practical." Don't use the word practical in any form of language. Don't use it. It's worse than a waste of time. You have to think about—do you want all babies to be born with the same characteristics from the date of birth to the end; do you want that? Are you content to seek that? Well, then you're not human; and that is a common characteristic of the average citizen of the United States. They have no comprehension of what the meaning of humanity is. They want to be practical.

And our organization suffers deeply from a spread of leanings toward being practical. If you're practical, you're incompetent; because you cannot achieve what's important, what has to be done right now, on the basis of being practical. You cannot say, "I'm being practical." That means you're an idiot; because if you have any talent, you're suffocating it.

The idea that we have practical standards of behavior for our organization has always been a piece of nonsense; that never worked. And we do have people who are able to cope with that challenge to some degree or other, but the way we have tended to do it—When somebody starts to make a suggestion, I want to leave the room. When people start telling me that they've got this practical idea that's got to be brought to the organization, I wish to leave the room. I don't like that at all, because if you can't create something which is useful and novel, you shouldn't talk. Without creativity, there's no manhood.

The organization has to bring itself up to a higher standard of performance and to the nature of the goals—what mankind is supposed to effect. And in general, in the organization, people cover over defects which should not be tolerated; it spoils the market.

Look, *you have to realize how dangerous this is!* This will be the summer months, and what have you got to deal with for those summer months? What skills do you have? What insight do you have? How are you going to make it work? Do you realize what's going on in the world now? What the war is, the great war? *China and Russia against the Nazis of the world?* Because most of our representatives are part of the Nazis of the world; in the United States, the leaders of the United States are mostly assholes of the world, or something less dignified. And that's what our problem is with our

kremlin.ru

President Vladimir Putin addressing attendees at the concert in liberated Palmyra, Syria, performed by the Mariinsky Theater Orchestra.

organization. We accept a standard of achievement which is below anything that will realize a truly necessary benefit for mankind.

The Purpose of Mankind

We do not have an approach presently, as an organization, the kind of approach which is necessary to make successful progress under these kinds of conditions. We do have available to us, if we think properly, we do have the ability to scratch into the things that we have to consider if we're going to be successful in defeating this problem.

You have to realize, we're on the edge of a virtual extinction of humanity in terms of the

CC/Svm-1977

The first major problem Putin had to deal with after becoming Prime Minister in 1999, was the mercenary attack against Russia in Chechnya. Here, the Zhani-Vedeno ambush attack on Russian forces in March 2000.

United States, in terms of Mexico; Mexico is really rotten as Hell. And we have no sign that there will be any improvement. Mexico once had a great mission; but then, the great mission was destroyed by the Wall Street crowd. So, there's no more of that. In the nations of South America, you find a degeneration of those economies which I had lived through in terms of experience over long years. Mankind has not yet become a successful creature; because we don't understand what the challenge of being a creature of that type means.

I could say many things about that, but that's what bothers me; it bothers me that people are inured in the kinds of ideas that really don't mean much of anything. *And what I'm doing is spending most of what is left of my life to try to save the cause of creativity, and it's a tough war to fight, because people don't believe in the kind of warfare that is necessary to succeed.*

That *is* the situation. That is the ongoing situation, right now. Look at it. The most recent event, which is this music celebration [in Palmyra]. That was an example that Putin *is* in charge now; this is not unique. I was in the same game, the *identical* same game when I was recovering from a serious illness; so I went out and ran this program I did, which was done with Putin. Not directly with Putin, but in concert with Putin.

But Putin picked up with me on exactly what I was

doing, and he's done it ever since then. And therefore, when you're trying to deal with this thing, this matter of how this thing is going to work, you've got to think about *that* and go back to that level. When Putin began organizing in a desolate area of work for him, I jumped in on it, too, on the Chechen issue, and we together were able to create an example; I did the demonstration of the thing, the Army moving up there—the Chechens. So, we have been doing that since then; the whole thing was what I was already doing—Helga [LaRouche] was in on it. What we did with the Russians was always on that basis, and that's what I'm talking about.

If you look at most of the people in the nations of Europe today, of Western Europe and trans-Atlantic Europe, you will find out they're idiots; they have no comprehension of what reality is. None. And that's what we've got. And I've got that factor which I expressed way back then, with Putin; that factor is the factor that you've got to look at. That is the defining factor; no gimmicks.

You have seen it several times already in recent times, what Putin was doing. Putin is the world's leading strategist in the world at this time. *And if you don't understand that, you don't know what this is all about.*

Look at Putin's strategy. Even in the recent period, Putin's strategy is always to solve a problem, to *solve* a problem, and to stop action at that point, and wait for

Michael Evans

A succession of presidents who were not incompetent was disrupted by assassination or attempted assassination. Left, President John Kennedy and Robert Kennedy; right, President Ronald Reagan.

the next action which is due to proper effect. And that is what does not exist with Obama. And people who are tied to Obama are leading the citizens of the United States into mass killing, mass death. Anyone who votes to support Obama or to support the leading candidates now, including Hillary, is doomed to destruction. I think this clown, this goon [Trump], is only another case of the same thing.

See, the point is that mankind is not a bunch of objects that you can manipulate and make the toys dance for you. That does not work. You have to actually create a power *in* mankind which is improved *over* previously existing expressions of mankind. That's the whole game. And you have to spread this kind of development, such that it sustains itself. Most people just don't have any idea what truth is. Because they think, *"Let's be practical."* The typical stupid person in the United States says, "let's be practical." And they're stupid. Whenever they take that attitude they are being stupid, ridiculous, disgusting.

Because the whole thing—the purpose of man is that mankind, in the process of developing the species, shall come to a capability to realize improvements, consistently building it up. You don't go to war to win a

war; you go to prevent, to destroy that which threatens mankind. But you have to get a net gain; you have to evoke a net gain.

Something Better than Ever Before

The ability of mankind to develop within the human individual the characteristics to be able to give a higher degree of power to mankind as a whole, through self-development of the human species—that's the *only* thing that's important.

The organization of the United States, it's a farce. It has no comprehension, it has no *desire* to achieve comprehension, and that's the most savage thing of it all! People wonder how to make something work that doesn't work, and that's where they failed. They say, "well, we're better than they are," or "we have failed on this," and "they have failed on this, but we're successful!" And think of what this has meant, ever since the FBI was brought into power in the United States.

The introduction of the FBI into the existence of the United States, was the death knell of the United States! And we had Presidents who were murdered on that basis. We have been unable to sustain any succession of Presidents who were not incompetent—or worse. Two brothers got killed. One was murdered in the South, and then the brother who was about to be named as nominee to become President, was killed on the evening before the nomination. And I've had serious involvement with this. What happened to Ronald Reagan? The Bushes tried to kill him! The Reagan administration, of which I was an integral part, was never able to be reconstructed.

And so you had garbage. I was the last key figure in this, when I was in a very particular training service for Ronald Reagan. But Ronald Reagan never had an opportunity to sustain what his policy was. What did you get? You got the Bushes *and Obama*. And Obama is worse than the Bushes.

Look at this whole campaign, now, the two Presidential tickets. That's why Putin's likely to win the whole thing, with his friends. And if we want to have

George W. Bush (left) was followed by Barrack Obama (right), who was even worse than Bush.

some part in that, we've got to look up and learn the lesson that this represents.

The key lies not in the personnel as such. It lies in the development of the personnel and development of the character of their behavior and their mission orientation. And that is the factor which wins the war! In other words, this is not a matter of a number of people who are fighting the war, not the ones who have gained this or gained that; that is not the issue. The issue is, can the human species produce from within its own ranks, a body of people who will meet the challenge of defeating the kind of evil we have to face now.

So when people say, "Well, he's going to win this war. He's going to win this war. He's going to win that war. He's going to win that war. He's going to win that war!" He's gonna lose that war! That's what the game is, and they're all playing that game! They don't have the ability to win, because they have not been given the *capability* to win, inside themselves.

And that's where the recent experience of Putin comes in. He has worked on a continuous drive to win the global war. And it's not to win the war in the sense of killing people; that was not the way he has functioned in his recent activities. *Not at all!* It's the *development of the individual* within the nation—*that* is the key to power. The ability to create something *better* than mankind has known and experienced beforehand.

So trying to win that and win that, and win this and win this,— it's all nonsense, it's for children, it's for masturbators.

What Really Happened in Syria

The importance of creativity is located in the development of the power of the human mind, and without that development of the human mind as such, there is nothing. And when I ridicule what we do in this organization, that's what I'm ridiculing. "You think you're so damned smart, you think that you won something. You think that you are so successful. You think that you had a better opinion than the other guy." That's exactly what *kills* mankind. Because it turns culture into some kind of monster, of evil. And you're so concerned to win a battle, to get ahead, to defeat people, to equip them, to promote them. Why? On the basis of their incompetence, which is the usual kind of thing that goes on in education, with respect to physical science and so forth. But what they promote is *pretension,* fatal pretension. They're trying to denounce things that should have been developed.

And that's what's wrong with this organization: *We have not grasped the urgent question of what wins.* Do you win by beating the other guy? Or is there something else? Is it not the development of the human person, in the human personality, where the human personality grows into something better than an individual? It's this pride about individualism,— that is the thing that causes the destruction of the members of our organization. They don't think about what the whole thing is about. And we're seeing it right now.

Question: Some of our best military contacts have

The greatness of the best military commanders, such as General Douglas MacArthur, is based on something internal to that person. Here, MacArthur wading ashore during initial landings at Leyte, Philippine Islands, in October 1944.

given a much more in-depth picture of how Putin organized his Syria victory, which you know, is incomplete but really very advanced. It's not just the air operations or the timing of the intervention. They completely reorganized a very demoralized Syrian military. They completely transformed it, down to the point that they assessed who were the most qualified Syrian commanders and put them in the most important front-line situations based on the strategy for victory. And it completely changed the character of the Syrian fighting force, in conjunction with what the Russians were doing. It was a concept of victory that had a lot of elements to it, that haven't even been made public yet.

LaRouche: It didn't work that way. It didn't work like that. It seemed to work that way. See, you had a bunch of people who were patriots, in terms of that institution, and they wanted to win the war for that reason. But that was only the local reason. The reason was they wanted to win *over* that war, to beat that war, to reject that war. So Putin came in, and Putin made it an effort which gave them the option of being successful.

When they had reached a point of achievement, where they were more or less independent of their temporary dependency on Putin, Putin pulled back. He didn't withdraw, but he pulled back and said, "You are

going through your own self-development now. Go out there and do it."

You've got to look at the question of where is the grace and glory of mankind to be located? In some person, in some trick? In some practice? No! It's in something *internal* to the person!—who realizes living in a certain way is what is to be achieved. And that's what the greatest commanders in military command have done—the same thing. MacArthur, for example, both he and his father—same thing. And that's what you'll find there.

Then what happened then? Well, the FBI, which was given power, turned the power over to itself, and produced leaders, military and other leaders, economic leaders in the United States, who degenerated the quality of the life of the human individual in the United States. And you can't tell me that I don't know that; I do know that. I know it perfectly. And I know that what that means to me is the degeneracy of the typical American! And the only way you're going to stop that is to tell the typical American, *"Stop being the typical American!"* And then go through a list of the kinds of things, the lies and the cheats that they do in the name of "success."

You've got to create beauty. You've got to create what's important. You've got to create mankind. You've got to fill mankind with greatness, so it is self-subjected to not doing anything that is not gracious. And that's why I make this point of criticism against the audience and here.

You cannot create heroes out of harlots.

This has always been the understanding of people who understood things, that creativity lies within the person who has allowed himself to assimilate creativity; not elsewhere. The desire is not to win, the desire is to create. And to do nothing that does not allow you to create. No, if you cannot infuse in human beings something that makes more human beings creative, then you have accomplished nothing. And that's the lesson. And I'll have more to say at a later date on this matter.

Every Day Counts In Today's Showdown To Save Civilization

II. Stop the War: Remove Obama

In the Face of World War III

by Dave Christie

"We are not on the edge of World War III. We are in the middle of it. We are already there, and if we don't stop it, civilization will no longer exist."

May 13—Lyndon LaRouche issued the above statement during the May 6 LaRouche PAC Friday Webcast, one day shy of the 71st year since the signing of the act of military surrender in Reims, France, marking the formal acceptance of Nazi Germany's unconditional surrender of its armed forces, by the Allies of World War II. Over the weekend after LaRouche spoke, and into the following Monday, May 9, "Immortal Regiment" marches would move through cities around the United States with a mixture of part solemnity, and mostly joy, celebrating the end of World War II and the defeat of fascism.

Yet, these celebrations were notably lacking the citizens whose relatives played such a decisive role: Namely, the citizens of the United States. Russians, and Americans of Russian (and other former USSR) descent, took to the streets in cities across the United States, as well as cities in other nations of the world. In Moscow, and other cities and towns across Russia, these celebrations of the victory over Fascism drew tens of thousands of participants. But, where were the Americans?

Why do Russians, and those of Russian heritage, have such a visceral sense of honoring those who fought the "Great Patriotic War," when most Americans can't even remember that Russia and China were our greatest allies in that war? Is it simply that the Soviet Union lost 27 million people in the war, while the United States only lost about half a million? Or, does it have something to do with the cultural difference between these nations?

Part of the answer lies in what Lyndon LaRouche has repeatedly identified as part of his personal experience after the war. While Lyndon LaRouche returned from World War II with a commitment to carry out Franklin D. Roosevelt's mission to continue the fight against fascist slavery, and free the world of the British Monarchy's "backward colonial policy," most of LaRouche's fellow veterans gave up the vision of FDR and capitulated to J. Edgar Hoover's FBI and Allen Dulles's CIA, which, together, ran a global assassination cartel to wipe out the leadership that shared Roosevelt's commitment to end the British colonial system.

The other part of the answer lies in the fact that

U.S. News & World Report/Library of Congress/Marion S. Trikosko

Most of Lyndon LaRouche's fellow military veterans capitulated to J. Edgar Hoover and Allen Dulles, and gave up FDR's post-World War II vision.

Russians have a far more acute sense of LaRouche's warning of the imminence of World War III. The Immortal Regiment is therefore not only a memorial for those who gave their lives in the past, but it is also a "living memorial" to honor that great mission to free the world from the grip of fascism. For many Russians now, there is a sense that fascism has returned. And whether it is in the form of Ukrainian Nazis or violent mercenaries under the cover of Islam, it has the same geopolitical intent, and the same sponsors: the British Monarchy.

kremlin.ru

President Vladimir Putin at the military parade in Red Square on May 9, 2016, marking the 71st anniversary of victory in the 1941-45 Great Patriotic War.

Putin Calls for a Non-Aligned System to Counter Terrorism

"Today our civilization has faced brutality and violence—terrorism has become a global threat," President Putin said to crowds in Moscow prior to the parade dedicated to the 71st anniversary of victory in World War II. *"We must defeat this evil, and Russia is open to join forces with all countries and is ready to work on the creation of a modern, non-aligned system of international security."*

According to the Russian leader, the lessons of the World War II showed that "double standards" and "short-sighted indulgence of those who are nurturing new criminal plans" are unacceptable.

"The lessons of history show that peace on our planet doesn't establish itself, that you need to be on high alert," he said.[1]

At the 2015 United Nations General Assembly this past September, Putin had issued the call for a coalition, "similar to the anti-Hitler coalition," to defeat the new fascist scourge of mercenary forces being deployed in the Southwest Asia:

What we actually propose is to be guided by common values and common interests rather than by ambitions. Relying on international law,

we must join efforts to address the problems that all of us are facing, and create a genuinely broad international coalition against terrorism. Similar to the anti-Hitler coalition, it could unite a broad range of parties willing to stand firm against those who, just like the Nazis, sow evil and hatred of humankind. And of course, Muslim nations should play a key role in such a coalition, since Islamic State not only poses a direct threat to them, but also tarnishes one of the greatest world religions with its atrocities. The ideologues of these extremists make a mockery of Islam and subvert its true humanist values.

Putin then asked, in an obvious reference to those who had signed the checks to these mercenaries:

"I'm urged to ask those who created this situation: do you at least realize now what you've done? But I'm afraid that this question will remain unanswered, because they have never abandoned their policy, which is based on arrogance, exceptionalism and impunity."[2]

'Islamic' Mercenaries and the Great Game

The use of paid mercenaries to destroy nations and spread barbarism is not a new concept. In fact, the re-

1. http://en.kremlin.ru/events/president/news/51890

2. http://en.kremlin.ru/events/president/news/50385

vival of the British Empire's *Great Game* of the Nineteenth Century was an instrumental feature of Winston Churchill's Iron Curtain which launched the "Cold War" and pitted the allies of World War II against each other, under the classic imperial policy of *"divide et impera."* Bernard Lewis, the British Foreign Office agent turned Princeton professor, trained a cadre of young naifs and fascists, many of whom became the inner core of the neo-conservatives working out of the U.S. Senate office of Lewis's friend Scoop Jackson (D-Wash.). Lewis also indoctrinated Zbigniew Brzezinski in his "Arc of Crisis" Great Game program, which became the core of the foreign policy of the Carter Administration. Under Brzezinski, mercenaries called the Mujahedeen were deployed against the Soviet Union in a form of proxy war, led by Osama bin Laden.

In 1999, as the newly sworn-in Prime Minister under President Boris Yeltsin, Vladimir Putin faced his first challenge in the form of the Second Chechen War. Chechnya had become the home base for the mercenaries who had sharpened their teeth fighting the Soviets in Afghanistan under Osama bin Laden. This war against Russia was supported by the American Committee for Peace in Chechnya (ACPC), which included Brzezinski and a menagerie of neocons, including Robert Kagan, whose wife Victoria Nuland continues to play, from within the Obama administration, a key role in the irregular warfare against Russia after her instrumental role in orchestrating the coup in Ukraine. In 1997, Kagan would found the Project for a New American Century (PNAC), which included many of the neocons from the ACPC, to explicitly prevent the emergence of what would be-

Standard You Tube License

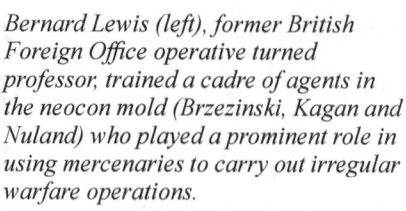

Bernard Lewis (left), former British Foreign Office operative turned professor, trained a cadre of agents in the neocon mold (Brzezinski, Kagan and Nuland) who played a prominent role in using mercenaries to carry out irregular warfare operations.

Zbigniew Brzezinski

CC/Mariusz Kubik

Victoria Nuland

Kleinschmidt/MSC

Robert Kagan

called the "multipolar" world by some foreign policy circles.

The Strategic Triangle & the BRICS

In October 2014, on the occasion of the 85th birthday of former Russian Prime Minister Yevgeny Primakov, Russian Foreign Minister Sergey Lavrov emphasized the importance of Primakov's role in creating the precursor to what is today known as the BRICS, which was the "Strategic Triangle" of Russia, India, and China, in the late 1990s. He said:

Russian artillery shelling mercenary fighters in Chechnya in January 2000.

British empire. In the early 1990s, while LaRouche was a political prisoner of the Bush Family and the "secret government" apparatus, his wife Helga Zepp-LaRouche was creating and organizing the New Silk Road concept, which is now unifying the Russia-India-China core of the BRICS process. The neocons behind the Project for a New American Century intended to crush this emerging new paradigm by lighting fires along the relevant borders of Russia, China, and India, calling for regime change and war in a list of nations that included Iraq, Iran, Yemen, Somalia, Libya, and Syria.

In a 1999 video presentation called *Storm Over Asia,* Lyndon LaRouche issued the warning that these British Empire-directed forces would use mercenaries under the banner of Islam to light small fires of conflict, that would spread to regional war, and ultimately to world war using nuclear weapons. In the video presentation, LaRouche said:

Remember that Yevgeny Primakov first set forth the idea of strengthening cooperation in the Russia-India-China (RIC) troika format, which jump-started the evolution of geopolitical structures advocating multi-polarity and the formation of a polycentric world, where all positions and rights are distributed in line with a [country's] actual economic and financial weight, as well as political clout. RIC became a pioneer in this respect. Eventually, BRIC was formed when Russia, India and China were joined by Brazil, and now it is BRICS, with the participation of the Republic of South Africa. There is a growing number of countries lining up to join this organization as full-fledged members or as dialogue partners.[3]

Primakov's Strategic Triangle concept was an integral part of the fight being waged by Lyndon LaRouche and his wife Helga Zepp-LaRouche to create a new system to replace the collapsing trans-Atlantic

U.S. Department of Defense/Robert D. Ward
Former Russian Prime Minister Yevgeny Primakov played a key role in establishing the Strategic Triangle of Russia, China, and India, the precursor of today's BRICS.

This war, if continued, using mercenaries, can lead to nuclear general war. The major powers principally threatened today by this mercenary operation, are two of the world's largest nations: China and India; China on its western borders, India on its northern borders. Iran is also threatened; but, more notably, Russia. If these nations are pushed to the wall by a continuing escalation of a war which is modelled on the wars which the British ran against Russia, China, and so forth, during the Nineteenth Century and early Twentieth Century, this will lead to the point that Russia has to make the decision to accept the disinte-

3. http://archive.mid.ru//brp_4.nsf/0/
B1EF6036BFC71092C3257D8000224D9D

In a 1999 video, LaRouche warned that British Empire directed mercenaries, posing as Islamic, would ignite conflicts that would prevent collaboration of the Strategic Triangle nations, and ultimately lead to nuclear war.

were seeking to overthrow the government of Syria. On Sept. 30, 2015, the upper house of the Russian Federal Assembly granted the request by Putin to deploy the Russian Air Force in Syria. For the next five and a half months, the Russian Air Force would conduct over 5,200 sorties to back up the ground forces of the Syrian government, and turn the tide in favor of the nation of Syria in the fight against the British-Saudi sponsored terrorists. The operation, which was formally ended March 14, 2016, cost $464 million, according to the Kremlin. This price tag is less than the $500 million paid for the failed program of Obama to train the "moderate" rebels in Syria to supposedly fight against ISIS, and orders of magnitude less than the trillions of dollars (estimated somewhere between $1 and 6 trillion) pumped into Obama's fraudulent "War on Terror."

On May 5, 2016, Putin launched another brilliant flank in Palmyra, with a concert performed by the St. Petersburg-based Mariinsky Theater Orchestra, led by world renowned conductor Valery Gergiev. The price tag of flying an orchestra into the middle of a war zone is unknown to this author, but could or should the effect of this concert be measured in mere monetary terms? How would you measure the value of the moralizing effect of bringing the beauty of Bach's Chaconne for Solo Violin into an ancient amphitheater, where just recently ISIS had carried out its barbaric beheadings?

Over the weekend following this historic cultural intervention in Palmyra, Immortal Regiment marches took place in forty-two countries, with over two million people participating around the world. As he had done in 2015, Putin again marched with a picture of his father, who had been severely wounded in World War II. LaRouche's associates were invited to march, sing, and speak at various locations around the United States, as well as in other countries. Long-time LaRouche PAC activist Al Korby, a veteran of World War II, was interviewed by the Russian news service TASS. In that interview, Korby stated, "We don't need any more wars,

gration of Russia as a nation, or to resort to the means it has, to exact terrible penalties on those who are attacking it, going closer and closer to the source, the forces behind the mercenaries— which include, of course, Turkey, which is a prime NATO asset being used as a cover for much of this mercenary operation in the North Caucasus and in Central Asia.[4]

LaRouche has stated that his policy approach was resonant with Putin's approach at the time of the war in Chechnya. That resonance has continued in many forms to this day, but above all, LaRouche has repeatedly emphasized that the current strategic flanking operations now being carried out by Putin are the primary reason we have not already entered into World War III.

Putin's Flanks

Within days of Putin's speech at last year's United Nations General Assembly, the Syrian Government formally approached Russia to ask for its help in combatting ISIS, al-Qaeda, and the other mercenaries that

—————————
4. http://archive.larouchepac.com/node/21709

and for that we must cooperate to develop space and new lands, and make scientific discoveries.... Americans should unite with Russians, both physically and spiritually, in ideas, and only then will there be no more wars."

The Ability to Create

Whether it is the march of the Immortal Regiment, or bringing beauty to the war-torn desert in a "Prayer for Palmyra," these actions represent a "living memorial," not simply to honor those who have sacrificed in the past, but as a living commitment to their posterity by continuing to fight now, for the future. Moreover, as flanking actions, they represent a quality of real power, with the potential to shift what might become possible in the days ahead. Lyndon LaRouche discussed the nature of this kind of power with some of his associates on May 10, and said that winning the war is not about killing people, but rather it is about developing the humanity of the individuals in your nation. LaRouche stated:

> And that's what the recent experience of Putin comes in. He has worked on a continuous drive to win the global war. And it's not to win the war in the sense of killing people; that was not the way he functioned in his recent activities. *Not at all!* It's the *development of the individual* within the nation—*that* is the key to power. The ability to create something *better* than mankind has known and experienced beforehand.

Obama does not understand the nature of this power. He only understands the power of the British Empire that he is subservient to, which grants him the power to kill and murder. In a recent *New York Times* article about Ben Rhodes, "The Aspiring Novelist Who Became Obama's Foreign Policy Guru," Rhodes provided a crucial psychological insight into how power is understood within the Obama Administration. To understand Obama, Rhodes said, one must grasp the critical influence of his upbringing and how that shaped his approach to "power" and "killings":

> Indonesia was a place where your interaction at that time with power was very intimate, right? Tens or hundreds of thousands of people had just been killed. Power was not some abstract

thing.... When we sit in Washington and debate foreign policy, it's like a "Risk" game, or it's all about us, or the human beings disappear from the decisions. But he [Obama] lived in a place where he was surrounded by people who had either perpetrated those acts—and by the way, may not have felt great about that—or else knew someone who was a victim. I don't think there's ever been an American president who had an experience like that at a young age of what power is.

> The parts of Obama's foreign policy that disturb some of his friends on the left, like drone strikes... are a result of Obama's particular kind of globalism, which understands the hard and at times absolute necessity of killing.

In this epic moment of human history, with a global financial collapse exacerbating the desperation of the British Empire, we don't have the time to wait and see whether someone who understands the "absolute necessity of killing," will follow orders or not. Obama must be removed, or thermonuclear war will follow.

A Moment of Truth for America And Her Citizens

by Jeffrey Steinberg and Robert Ingraham

May 17—The fifteen year cover-up of the truth about the Sept. 11, 2001 attacks on the World Trade Center and the Pentagon, in which 2,977 innocent people were killed, is now close to full exposure. Two successive American presidents—George W. Bush and Barack Obama—have lied and covered up the truth: The British-Saudi allies of the Bush-Cheney Administration pulled off the biggest terrorist attack on U.S. soil in history, murdering thousands of Americans in cold blood, and up until this very moment, agencies of the U.S. government, from the President to the FBI, have been complicit in the coverup of this crime.

We have now arrived at a moment where the truth threatens to emerge. What has made this possible, more than any other contributing factor, has been the dramatic shift in the global strategic environment, accomplished in the last six months as a result of the decision by Russian President Vladimir Putin to intervene directly into Syria against the British-Obama-Saudi terrorist apparatus. That intervention "broke all of the rules of the game," and revealed to all of the world the truth about the true sponsors of al-Qaeda, ISIS and the terrorist apparatus.

And in Washington, just as we were going to press today, the U.S. Senate passed the "Justice Against Sponsors of Terrorism Act," or JASTA, by unanimous voice vote, despite Obama's threat to veto it. This will allow 9/11 victims to sue Saudi Arabia. Hearings are expected in the House of Representatives in the near future.

At the same time, this past week, millions of Russians, and others, marched in *Immortal Regiment* victory celebrations, commemorating VE Day, the defeat of the Nazis 71 years ago. In Moscow, Vladimir Putin called for a nonaligned system of international security to counter global terror. And, on May 5, Russia's Mariinsky Theater Orchestra, led by Valery Gergiev, performed the works of Bach, Prokoviev, and others in a symphony concert, "Praying for Palmyra," at Palmyra's Roman Theater where ISIS had tortured and killed twenty-five people in 2015.

U.S. Navy Photo/Preston Keres

A New York City fireman calls for 10 more rescue workers to make their way into the rubble of the World Trade Center.

The shattering of the "controlled environment" of the past fifteen years, the threat that all of the trees in the forest could now fall, is seen explicitly in the naming of Lyndon LaRouche in a barrage of media attacks, which have appeared "out of the blue" in recent days.

On May 15, the *New York Times* suddenly attacked LaRouche, as "a world class conspiracy theorist, who … propounds a cracked and erudite worldview that has included Aristotle, John Maynard Keynes, Werner Heisenberg, and Timothy Leary—all linked through an internal logic that makes, for its believers, a scary kind of sense." Other attacks on LaRouche have appeared in newspapers ranging from Texas to California, from media which prefer to impose, under normal circumstances, an absolute blackout on anything to do with LaRouche or his movement.

LaRouche responded at his May 14 Manhattan Town Meeting:

What has happened is, that what we have managed to introduce, with the aid of the action by Putin, because everybody knows, internationally, what my relationship is, the silent relationship between Putin and me.… And what you saw, recently, from Putin's leadership, you saw that this is what has scared the unholy you-know-what-stuff.… Putin has suddenly been exposed as the greatest danger to Satan on the planet. Or maybe Satan was frightened, I don't know. And they are getting some of that fear of me, to be a fear in defense of Satan… remember, back before I was capped into prison, that was the last time they really went after me. They thought it was all fixed. Now recently, they've had a new reaction: they're terrified of me. And

Official portrait
Former FBI Director Louis Freeh

Official portrait
Former FBI Director Robert Mueller

that tells you what the score is. The score is Putin.

What's happened is that the forces of evil in Europe, have recognized that Putin is on top. He's on top in terms of the threat of warfare! It has been demonstrated repeatedly, and it's been finally recognized that Putin remembers what was done to his family, and he's sticking to the cause, not to get revenge, but to get victory. And that's where it is.

The 28 Pages

The fight to declassify the 28-page chapter from the original Joint Congressional Inquiry final report, which was completed in 2002, has reached the point where President Obama is now under immense pressure to make those pages public. While the exact content of the 28 pages is known only to its authors and to the more than 100 Members of Congress who have read them, it is more broadly known that they detail the role of officials of the Saudi government, the Royal Family, Saudi religious "charities" and front companies for the Saudi Ministry of Defense and Aviation, in aiding and abetting the hijackers.

What is revealed in those pages, however, is just the tip of the iceberg. 80,000-plus pages of FBI files have been hidden from the public and even from the Joint Inquiry and the later 9/11 Commission, detailing the role of a wealthy Saudi family with close business ties to the Royals, in facilitating the activities of a cell of 9/11 hijackers in Sarasota, Florida, including the "ringleader" Mohammed Atta. Just as the 28 pages detail the support from Saudi officials to the lead hijackers in San Diego, California, there are other investigations yet to be started in Falls Church, Virginia, Paterson, New Jersey and Boston, Massachusetts, as well as parts unknown.

Two former FBI Directors—Louis Freeh and Robert Mueller—have led the cover-up. Mueller, who headed the FBI at the time of the 9/11 attacks, spent more time meeting with 9/11 Commissioners than any other public official, and his objective was to bury the 28 pages and conceal the direct role of the FBI in facilitating the attacks, whether by gross incompetence, or worse, complicity. Freeh left the FBI to become the personal attorney of Saudi Prince Bandar bin-Sultan, aka "Bandar Bush," who personally funded at least two of the hijackers and was the key player in the Al-Yamamah deal, which established the massive offshore Anglo-Saudi slush funds for global terrorism.

Obama Lies

At the time of this writing, it is known that members of the Obama Administration are frantic to stop the momentum for the truth to come out, and they are attempting to sucker key Democrats, as well as families of the 9/11 victims, into the belief that Obama will "do the right thing." At a recent Capitol Hill reception, leading Congressional Democrats reported that President Obama has personally promised to release the 28 pages "in some form." However, sources close to the Obama White House report that this is a total lie, and Obama is committed to protecting his British and Saudi sponsors to his last moment in office.

That reality has been made public in recent weeks. CIA Director John Brennan has been deployed as the national point man, by Obama, to attack those individuals demanding full disclosure. As part of this, he went on national television, only one week after the 60 Minutes broadcast promoting the release of the 28 pages, and lied that the 28 pages were debunked by the 9/11 Commission. White House spokesman Josh Earnest has also repeatedly seconded Brennan's blatant lies.

Challenging the Silent Acquiescence to Evil

On May 16, Lyndon LaRouche took part in a dialogue with the LaRouche PAC Policy Committee, which was broadcast live. On the subject of 9/11, he had the following to say:

LaRouche: "You see on the burning out of the towers, in the southern tip of Manhattan, and this thing was *awful*. And I was actually looking at this thing, by a television transmission of what was happening in the process. I was familiar with those two towers. I had lived in that area, and I knew what was in the area. So when I was recalling this process, as it was being presented live in the burning out of these two towers, you had a gripping feeling about the whole business.

"But the thing, when *Obama* came into this picture and became a supporter of this with the Bushes, *then* you had to become alive. You had to realize what the truth was. And for the people of Manhattan... suddenly, in the later period, people would look back at it, shudder about it, not want to think about it, and to say, 'No. No, no, no, forget it. Don't discuss that, don't discuss that, don't discuss that.' And that's where the problem lies.

"We have similar things. We avoid recognizing things that are true, but decide to conceal them, because you don't want to have to share recollection of them. And that's what was happening. The culture of the United States, as of now, will depend upon whether or not—and remember I was a witness to this whole process: The first plane comes in. What's in the plane? Well, passengers. What are the passengers doing? The passengers are being driven to death. One after the other, driven to death. And then you had other phases of the death process, on the same thing....

"So this is current time. And *nothing was ever done*, so far, to rectify what happened in that effect. And other things were correlatives of the same thing, what they were doing, what their effect was, how people responded, how the members of Congress responded. How the officials of the government otherwise, how did they respond? They all have the same guilty knowledge, in their own way. And therefore, they acquired of themselves, the quality of something that is redolent of Satan.

"And this is something that happened in America. It happened by the ruling forces of the United States who conceded to the British, and to the Saudi associates of the British. That's what happened. And the whole thing *did* happen: *It was horrible!* And the conscience of people who have any understanding of this, would mostly try to hide from this, avoid it, don't recognize it—Don't look! Don't look! Don't look! Don't look! And that's where we are now. The question is, are we going to look, or not?"

The AfD Party: Old Wine In New Bottles?

by Helga Zepp-LaRouche, chairman of the German political party BüSo

The tidal wave of refugees entering Europe from the Middle East and Africa—as a result of Obama's destructive wars on behalf of British policy—in the context of Europe's economic collapse as a result of the demands of the banks, has enabled the rise of a new party of dissent in Germany, the Alternative für Deutschland *(AfD). Zepp-LaRouche asks, What is it, and why?*

May 13—The crucial question for many people in Germany today is not where do you stand on religion, but where do you stand on the Alternative for Germany (AfD)? Is it only a "party of people in a bad mood," which we should not describe as Nazis as long as the AfD is "only right-wing populist," as the deputy chairman of the SPD Olaf Scholz put it? Where could Chancellor Angela Merkel have seen people "frothing at the mouth" when they confront the AfD? Does the AfD really provide the "light at the end of the tunnel," because it denies the influence of CO_2 emissions on the climate, as AfD member Michael Limburg, who is Vice President of the European Institute for Climate and Energy (EIKE), puts it? The presence of varying currents within it, and its sudden electoral successes, make it appear that the most diverse expectations and forms of wishful thinking can be projected onto the AfD.

So what should we think about this party? Can its program fulfill the hopes of those who have voted for it? Is it dangerous, or can it develop into something dangerous? Does it have solutions for today's existential challenges, such as the escalating danger of a new, this-time-thermonuclear world war, or for the acute danger of a new financial collapse of the trans-Atlantic sector, much more dramatic this time than in 2008, or—to mention one issue that the AfD has already addressed—does it have a solution for the refugee crisis?

Since the party's self-conception rules out any attempt at strategic thinking, it is foreign to the AfD to attempt to define a solution to overcome the war danger. Since the party is completely trapped in a diffuse mix of social liberalism and the Austrian School, it does not have the analytical prerequisites needed to recognize the magnitude of the crisis, let alone a conception of how to overcome the systemic crisis of the trans-Atlantic financial system.

And even on the refugee crisis, a subject on which the AfD expects to be attractive, its incompetence is appalling. This is the greatest humanitarian catastrophe since the immediate post-war period; there will be many hundreds of millions of people fleeing war, starvation, and epidemics in the years to come, if the causes

ruptlyTV/you tube

Frauke Petry, shown here July 4, 2015, was elected the new chair of Alternative für Deutschland, with 59.7% of the vote.

of refugee flight are not resolved. Whoever believes that this crisis can be solved by stopping refugees at the borders with barbed wire and firearms, and purports to implement such a plan, is not only deceiving himself and others, but accepts the hateful spirit of the authors of such proposals.

Rage at the Establishment

Any classification of this party must begin by defining what lies behind its sudden leap in popularity. The source is the complete policy failure of the European Union (EU), the German

EIRNS/Ilya Karpowski

A closed-down, decaying factory in Berlin (2006).

government, and the established parties, which for a considerable time have given a growing share of the population the impression that there is ultimately no authority that takes their interests to heart or to which they can turn. And as long as this is not admitted and corrected, the major parties will continue to shrink. Mrs. Merkel has occasionally said that the fundamental causes of the refugee crisis must be addressed, but she has not done so: She has addressed neither the wars of the Bush and Obama regimes, based on lies, in Iraq, Afghanistan, Libya, Syria and Yemen—one cause of the refugee crisis—nor the IMF policy of denying credit to Africa, thus prohibiting any economic development—another cause. As a result, these causes, as well as a real approach for solving the problem, are not understood. That is why more and more citizens fall for the simplistic, incompetent, and profoundly inhuman proposals of the AfD.

The more the German government and the legislature, the Bundestag, have ceded competences and responsibility to a untransparent, soulless bureaucracy in Brussels through European Union treaties from Maastricht to Lisbon, the more the feeling of helplessness grows, as expressed in the Germans' favorite saying: "You can't do anything about it!" The impression is thereby created that the party system doesn't allow the individual to influence political events in any way, because the criteria for nominating candidates and party discipline permit total control from the top. This control is exercised entirely for the benefit of financial interests and against the general welfare—as citizens have learned from experience—and as a result, the rich get richer and the shrinking middle class and the poor get ever poorer, especially since 2008 and the repeated "rescue packages." *Handelsblatt*, for example, recently published documentation of what was already clear: 95% of the rescue packages for Greece flowed into the European banks.

Consider these conditions: The implementation of Hartz 4 (the latest phase of the Hartz commission's reforms of labor policy), amounting to the cold-hearted expropriation of people unemployed through no fault of their own; the flop of the supplementary pension plan (the Riester pension); poverty among the elderly; rising costs and worsening care in health care; the lack of affordable housing; a growing sense of insecurity due in part to layoffs of police; the feeling of being left alone in encountering cultures of immigrant communities that you don't understand; the feeling of being manipulated by the mass media, of not being protected by the government from total surveillance by domestic and foreign intelligence services; and the awareness that your government is being led by the nose by the United States and Great Britain into a confrontational policy against Russia and China, which is provoking a new war danger. The list could be significantly longer. The result is that more and more people do not feel represented by the established parties. That is not only the case in Germany, but in most European countries and the United States—take the case of Donald Trump, for example.

Learn from History

In Germany, this development presents very obvious parallels to the situation in the 1920s and 1930s: The debt demands of the Versailles Treaty were in essence the same as the EU debt-corset today, which puts the interests of the profit-seeking casino bankers above those of the general welfare, whether in Greece or Germany. The difference between Brüning and Schacht, on the one side [German Chancellor and Reichsbank President in the period before Hitler], and today's Schäuble and Draghi on the other [German Finance Minister and European Central Bank President], lies only in the predicates, not in the fundamentals. It is almost lawful that various political and social movements, out of a very similar frustration and lack of trust in the political system, are expressing themselves in similar forms.

And precisely as in that time, one can very clearly differentiate between the many who—feeling uprooted and betrayed—follow anyone who promises pragmatic solutions in ideological wrapping, and those who, as masterminds of geopolitical interests, understand how to use the social ferment for their own objectives.

The key to understanding the process which characterized the run-up to the First World War—as well as the developments between the world wars—and which has today brought about these processes in the United States, Europe, and even in Germany in respect to the AfD, is the continuing tradition of the Conservative Revolution. This is a reaction against the "ideas of 1789," that is, against the ideas of the French Revolution, and even more so, against the Leibniz-oriented American Revolution, of universal human rights, and an image of man which understands the individual as capable of limitless perfectability.

Then, as today, this Conservative Revolution—to which "right-wing intellectuals" such as today's Götz Kubitschek refer—was not a homogenous world outlook, but a broad spectrum of ethnic nationalist ("völkisch") and "national revolutionary" ideologies, but always exclusionary, backward, and based on defining mankind by his biology.

To come straight to the point: If we have learned anything from history, then we should see the difference between how America got out of the Depression and the world economic and financial crisis of the 1930s, and what happened in Europe. In America, President Franklin D. Roosevelt ended the casino economy which was responsible for the crisis. He did it with the Glass-Steagall banking separation law, the reintroduction of the credit system based on Alexander Hamilton, the Reconstruction Finance Corporation, the Tennessee Valley program, and later his own plan for the Bretton Woods System, altogether a package of measures that brought America out of the crisis and allowed it to become the world's strongest economic power. In Europe, by contrast, varied forms of fascism prevailed, from Mussolini to Franco, Petain, and Hitler.

It is an irony of history that today China, with its policy of the New Silk Road, is implementing the Franklin Roosevelt tradition, while America, in the grip of Wall Street, advocates recipes taken out of mothballs from the Europe of the 1930s. Germany is still teetering on the brink: It has not yet decided which pathway to take. *(To be continued.)*

YEMEN

Readings of *EIR* World Land-Bridge Report Become National Events

No, there is a limit to the tyrant's power,
When the oppressed can find no justice, when
The burden grows unbearable—he reaches
With hopeful courage up unto the heavens
And seizes hither his eternal rights,
Which hang above, inalienable
And indestructible as the stars themselves.

—The opening lines of the Rütli Oath, from Friedrich Schiller's drama of freedom, Wilhelm Tell, *a stunning demonstration that uplifting the self-identity of a people to a higher image of mankind is the only basis for victory against an adversary whose actions are self-limited to satanic, dehumanizing, brute force.*

May 13—Since March 23 of this year, the Advisory Office for Coordination with the BRICS, a Yemen-based organization headed by Fouad al-Ghaffari, has conducted a series of enormously successful weekly reading sessions of the Arabic translation of the *EIR* Special Report, "The New Silk Road Becomes the World Land-Bridge," in the capital city of Sanaa. These sessions have quickly developed into na-

tional events, with the participation of government ministers, universities, poets, intellectuals, businesses, civil society organizations, and the most prominent national and international mass media outlets. To further expand this national dialogue process, 1,000 copies of the report were printed this past week for distribution among institutions and individual citizens.

These high-level deliberations on the future that the citizen-intellectuals of Yemen strive to create for themselves, in cooperation with the BRICS, have become a

courtesy of Hussein Askary

Dr. Abdul Aziz al-Magaleh (left), a poet and former President of Sana'a University, now the Head of the Center for Studies and Research in Yemen, receiving an Arabic-language copy of the Land-Bridge Report from Abdulmalik al-Qaefi, Advisor to the Advisory Office for Coordination with the BRICS, in Sana'a, Yemen on May 10, on the occasion of the eighth weekly reading session of the EIR report The New Silk Road becomes the World Land-Bridge. *All the others in the photo are also associated with the Advisory Office for Coordination with the BRICS, in Yemen.*

source of optimism for the potential to relaunch a reconciliation process to establish peace and rebuild the country, despite the ongoing Anglo-American-Saudi genocidal assault on the nation that continues to this day.

On May 10, the 8th session was held to read Part 3 of the report, "China: Silk Road to Development and Peace," and was attended and addressed by acting Minister of Communications Mr. Muslih Muhsin al-Azir. The meeting was also attended by the Chairman of the Yemeni Center for Strategic Studies and Research, Dr. Abdul-Aziz al-Muqalih, one of the best known Yemeni poets and novelists, and by another prominent poet, al-Gharbi Amran. Copies of the freshly printed report were presented as gifts to some of the prominent guests. A large banner, featuring an image of the report's cover, the map of the World Land-Bridge from the back cover, and a portrait of China's President Xi Jinping, adorned the background banner of the meeting.

Hussein Askary, co-author of the *EIR* report and translator of the Arabic version, addressed the meeting by video and explained the Chinese role in the New Silk Road, which—according to Helga Zepp-LaRouche, Chairwoman of the Schiller Institutes and New Silk Road Lady—is "history's greatest peace and development project."

Return to Nuclear Power

Askary explained the history of the joint Schiller Institute/Chinese efforts to promote and build this project since at least 1996. He explained the three main pillars of the Confucian philosophy behind the New Silk Road—love, harmony, and mutual benefit—and that these are diametrically opposed to the current, destructive and inhuman Anglo-American system.

Acting Minister al-Azir lauded the historic ties between Yemen and China that extend from the pre-Islamic period (pre-7th Century AD), China's support for the people of Yemen since the republican revolution of 1962, and its support for aspects of development of which every Yemeni citizen feels the impact, especially the Sanaa-Hudaida highway. Al-Azir also stressed the importance of enhancing the good relations with the People's Republic of China and praised the Advisory Board for Coordination with BRICS for improving Yemen's relations with friendly nations such as China.

On May 9, the Advisory Office had held a joint event in the University of Sanaa and its affiliated Center for Strategic Research to sign a protocol of cooperation on the New Silk Road report and other research related to it.

Previous reading sessions dealt with the physical economic ideas of Lyndon LaRouche included in Part 2, "Metrics of Progress." Following discussion of the importance of nuclear power, the Deputy Minister of Electricity and Energy, Dr. Hareth al-Amri, stated that the Yemeni government should revive its nuclear power program, which was abandoned in the 1990s.

In the Midst of War

Media coverage of these events has been constant, and interest in the New Silk Road and the connection of Yemen to both the Economic Belt of the New Silk Road and the 21st Century Maritime Silk Road has been awakened massively in the country, especially through understanding the importance of this vision and these ideas for the reconstruction of Yemen after the ongoing, devastating war, in which Saudi warplanes, firing American and British weapons, focus on destroying the basic infrastructure and industry, to force the people to kneel before the might of the British Empire. But that has not happened.

These Land-Bridge activities have also become a source of hope for the people of Yemen, who are suffering mightily in this satanic, geopolitical war. At the moment negotiations are under way in Kuwait under the auspices of the United Nations, between the Sanaa-based national forces, and the Saudi-backed government-in-exile. The Russian-Chinese efforts to put an end to the war in Syria and rebuild that country are also felt in the negotiations in Kuwait. The parties are being pressured from all sides to end the fighting and restore the political process which was progressing well, before the Saudis sabotaged it in March-April 2015.

Whatever the outcome of these negotiations, and whatever government is eventually established, it will have to take into consideration that the ideas embodied in the *EIR* Special Report, and the vision which the Yemenis are creating from their reading of these ideas, will be the basis for rebuilding the country and bringing peace and development to its current and future generations. China and Russia will contribute to this vision with their support and leverage, because the fate of Yemen will have a great impact on the way the New Silk Road peace project will go.

What a Brave and Beautiful New World!

Mohammed Aref reviews the Arabic translation of The New Silk Road Becomes the World Land-Bridge *for* Al-Ittihad, *Abu Dhabi, UAE.*

May 12—The Nicaraguan Canal will extend from the mouth of the Brito River on the Pacific Ocean to the mouth of the Punta Gorda River on the Atlantic Ocean. The maps for this 278 kilometer canal were prepared by American engineers 118 years ago, and Nicaragua launched its building in 2014. The canal project, which is expected to be completed in five years, includes two ports, an international airport, and cement and steel plants. It is one of the 27 such projects that make up the "World Land-Bridge network" through corridors, tunnels, and channels that connect the continents.

The deepest and longest rail tunnel is the Saikan Tunnel, which is 54 km long and 100 meters deep below the seabed, and connects the Japanese island Honshu to mainland Japan. But it will be surpassed by the Bohai underwater tunnel in China with a length of 100 km, which will be fitted with railways for high-speed trains between two Chinese industrial cities, Dalian and Yantai, with a population of 7 million people each. When completed in 2020, this tunnel will be the world's longest.

And what a beautiful, new world that built the Bosporus Tunnel under the Istanbul Strait for railway connection between Asia and Europe, which currently transports 3 million passengers daily. It is 14 km long and includes the deepest immersed-tube structure in the world. The proposal to build this tunnel was made in 1869, but was not built until 2013, and is described as the Iron Silk Road, in reference to the Silk Road which linked East Asia to the Arab world and Europe more than a thousand years ago.

On the other side of the Islamic world, the world's longest bridge is being built now, the Strait of Malacca Bridge, which will connect Malaysia to Indonesia, and will have a total length of 71 km.

And what a brave world is being planned now, at a time when emotions are swelling about the million-man immigration across the Mediterranean. The map of the Italy-Tunisia Connection includes the construction of four artificial islands in the Mediterranean to connect mainland Italy to Sicily, and Sicily to Tunisia across 155 km of the Mediterranean Sea, through the world's longest suspension bridge and five tunnels for passenger and cargo transport in both directions. While Washington is spending trillions of dollars to destroy physical and spiritual bridges between nations and peoples, the Egyptians dug the second Suez Canal in 2015, which will include a gigantic, world-class logistics hub. It will reduce the transit time of ships from eleven hours to three. The Egyptian people contributed $8 billion to finance this canal, which is considered a breakthrough in the financing of infrastructure through national credit rather than foreign credit.

The New Silk Road Becomes the World Land-Bridge is the title of a book that includes 200 maps, and whose Arabic translation was launched at an event at the Egyptian Transportation Ministry under the auspices of Minister Saad El-Geyoushi in March. In the headquarters of the Suez Canal Authority, Hussein Askary, the Iraqi researcher, co-author of the book and the translator of the Arabic version, lectured on the concept of the "development corridors" that enrich nations, while the "economy of geopolitics," which is based on enslavement and displacement, is staggering on the verge of collapse.

Although most of the authors of the book are Americans, the book itself is a guideline for a new world order in which Russia, China, and the BRICS will play the leadership role. The book relies on the "physical economics" developed by American economist Lyndon LaRouche, through which he challenges the "casino economy" whose "financial derivatives bubble" has reached $2 quadrillions (which means the number 2 with 15 zeros to its right) and could explode at any moment and put an end to the global financial system. LaRouche is a brave scientist and philosopher who ran for president of the United States four times. While current candidate Donald Trump is taking sides with the Zionist Lobby and the American Israel Political Action Committee (AIPAC), LaRouche exposed the latter in his campaigns, and in a book that eventually landed him in prison. While in prison, LaRouche wrote the book, *So, You Wish to Learn All about Economics,* which has been published in Arabic translation.

Translated from Arabic by Hussein Askary.

HELGA ZEPP-LAROUCHE

'Looking at the Map of Africa, One Can See That It Lacks Basic Infrastructure'

This interview of Helga Zepp-LaRouche was conducted for the weekly Cameroonian publication Intégration *on May 6 by its New York City correspondent Celestin Ngoa Balla, and was published in its May 16 issue. Below is a transcript of the interview.*

May 6—The political activist answers the questions of the newspaper *Intégration* after the April 7 conference of the Schiller Institute in New York City.

Intégration: You just held a conference in New York. What was it about? What was said there? And what should we expect next?

Helga Zepp-LaRouche: In this New York conference we focussed on the war danger and the fantastic breakthroughs of the New Silk Road development in various countries, the science of the future, and the dialogue of cultures. The best is, you go on our websites and look at it yourself. And we will do more of these kinds of events.

http://www.schillerinstitute.org/
http://newparadigm.schillerinstitute.com/

Intégration: You have been lecturing all around the world, but never in black Africa and, in particular, never in Cameroon. So when will you visit us?

Helga Zepp-LaRouche: I have been in conferences in Khartoum and Abuja. I have been working on African development programs since the beginning of the 1970s, so it is not a lack of interest, but of opportunity.

Intégration: Why are you calling for a New World Economic Order?

Helga Zepp-LaRouche: Because the present world order, which is generally called "globalization," is completely bankrupt, financially as well as morally. The need for a just New World Economic Order is today much more urgent than it was half a century ago, when the Nonaligned Movement demanded a New World Economic Order. The great humanitarian crisis, which is reflected in the fact that millions and millions of people are fleeing today from war, hunger, and poverty from Southwest Asia and Africa, and are risking their lives in trying to get to Europe, which is closing its borders, is a condemnation of those who try to maintain a system which only benefits a few, and sacrifices billions. Mankind has reached a crossroads, where either we define a new paradigm which takes into account the interest of all human beings living on this planet, or we will plunge even deeper into a new dark age, or even a third world war.

Intégration: Doesn't the International Conference on Corruption indicate some guidelines for this new World Economic Order?

Helga Zepp-LaRouche: I can't see that this conference has done anything in practice to change the corruption of the present system. Just take the enormous multitude of crimes the trans-Atlantic banking system is involved in, as revealed by the so-called "Panama Papers," where the banks organized systematic tax evasion and other illegal activities, which is only the tip of the iceberg. Or the Libor rate manipulation, swindling people out of three digit sums of billions, or the drug money laundering of such banks as HSBC. These guidelines so far are only words.

Intégration: You are saying that we should expect regime changes in many countries, particularly in Africa where we see the phenomenon of "Presidents for life" who are able to avoid any recourse to democracy?

Helga Zepp-LaRouche: The tragedy is that in Africa many leaders who fought for the common good of their people were assassinated and replaced by stooges for the colonial system, which in a way still exists, for example in the form of the conditionalities of the IMF. In his book *The Economic Hitman* John Perkins describes very well how this system operates still today. One also has to see that the nice sounding words "democracy" and "human rights" have often become a synonym for foreign interventions to bring to power people who would fulfill the interest of the trans-Atlantic financial system.

Intégration: Cameroon head of state M. Paul Biya has often called for a Marshall plan for Africa. Do you think that this is necessary and possible?

Helga Zepp-LaRouche: Absolutely! It is more than necessary, given the extreme poverty in many areas and countries in Africa. It is also a realistic possibility for the near future. China has started to build the New Silk Road and Maritime Silk Road, where already more than 60 countries are cooperating. My organisation, the Schiller Institute, has produced a 370-page study, describing how The New Silk Road Becomes the World Land Bridge, which has a large section on key development projects for Africa, which would be a complete game changer. Primarily, large infrastructure projects are the absolute precondition for the development of agriculture and industries, as well as water projects, energy production and distribution, and new cities.

However, I would not call it a Marshall Plan, because the New Silk Road extended into Africa should not have a cold war connotation, but be a win-win perspective for all participants.

Intégration: The international press gave you the nickname of "Silk Road Lady." How do you justify this name and what exactly is the Silk Road initiative?

Helga Zepp-LaRouche: I guess I got that nickname, because I have campaigned now for 25 years for the New Silk Road, because that is what my husband and I proposed when the Soviet Union disintegrated in 1991. Then we called it the "Eurasian Land-Bridge/New Silk Road," which was the proposal to connect the population and industrial centers of Europe and Asia through development corridors, opening up the landlocked areas of the Eurasian continent. We have conducted literally hundreds of conferences and seminars on this topic all over the world since.

The good news is that in 2013 Chinese President Xi Jinping announced the New Silk Road as the official policy of China in the tradition of the ancient Silk Road, uniting peoples through an exchange of goods, technol-ogies, cultures, and ideas. In the two and a half years since then, this project has taken on an enormous momentum, and it is right now the only positive perspective on the planet.

Intégration: We have to ask you, what does the new Silk Road initiative mean for Africa, or what contribution can Africa make to the New Silk Road initiative?

Helga Zepp-LaRouche: If you look at the map of Africa, you can see that it lacks basic infrastructure. The few railway lines and roads still are not much better than they were during colonial times, when they were built only to exploit raw materials. So essentially it would mean building integrated high-speed railways, highways, waterways, as well as investment in advanced technologies and education. This would not only provide for the elimination of poverty, hunger and disease in a very short time, but also leapfrogging as quickly as possible to the most advanced technologies, to learn the lesson from the Chinese economic model, which has brought about the most spectacular economic miracle in the last 25 years. This model is based on exactly the same economic theory which was also the basis for the German economic model in the postwar period in Germany. In principle, this model can be replicated everywhere, if one focuses on the best possible education of the population and brings forward its creativity.

Africa can contribute its enormous human potential to the development of mankind as a whole. The more people study the projects and the philosophy of the New Silk Road, the quicker it can be put on the agenda. In some countries there are already study groups that get together once or twice a week, and they study the theory of physical economy which goes back to Gottfried Wilhelm Leibniz, and which has been developed further by my husband Lyndon LaRouche.

Intégration: Why are you always warning that a third world war is imminent? Who would benefit from such a catastrophe?

Helga Zepp-LaRouche: As everybody can easily see, the United States and NATO are presently engaged in a policy of encirclement against Russia and China, which is reaching a very dangerous point. The reason is that the trans-Atlantic financial system is completely bankrupt, and some oligarchical circles see their power threatened by the rise of China.

Nobody would benefit from a third world war with thermonuclear weapons which would lead to the extinction of the human species.

Intégration: And the remedy you propose is what you call a "cultural and scientific renaissance"?

Helga Zepp-LaRouche: You also need a new financial system, replacing the present bankrupt one with a credit system, by implementing the Glass-Steagall banking separation, which was introduced by F.D. Roosevelt.

But the new economic order will only function if you change the present culture, which is mostly evil and ugly, and which shapes the thinking of people in a very destructive way.

We must revive the best tradition of each culture and than have a dialogue between the best expression of each civilization and culture. That way people start to learn about each other, chauvinism and xenophobia disappear, and out of this revival then the ground is being laid to create a new renaissance.

Intégration: How does this scientific and cultural renaissance manifest itself? What part does Africa play in it?

Helga Zepp-LaRouche: There are clear frontiers of science which will lead to a completely new platform of economic activity. One such area is the research into thermonuclear fusion. Breakthroughs can be expected in the short term, both in respect to the stellarator model in Greifswald in Germany, where in February scientists succeeded producing a plasma at several million degrees Celsius for the tenth of a second and where the goal is to reach a stable plasma for 30 minutes much hotter than our sun by the year 2020, and also concerning a recent breakthrough at a different reactor type in China, at the Experimental Advanced Superconducting Tokamak (EAST) at the Institute of Physical Science in Hefei, recently. A fusion based economy means energy and raw-material security for all of mankind. Another area is space research and travel.

A cultural renaissance would indicate that society is finally becoming human again, as it was in the past only during brief periods, such as Gupta period in India, certain dynasties, such as the Song dynasty in China, the Abbasid period in the Arab world, the Italian Renaissance, the Golden Age of Timbuktu, or the German classical period. A new renaissance would mean, that that kind of thinking would be the standard and basis for new breakthroughs of creativity in all areas of science and culture.

EIR

Construction of a water-transfer project, moving 5% of the water in the Congo River to rapidly disappearing Lake Chad, is one EIR proposal to create much needed infrastructure in Africa. Other EIR proposals have included extensive high-speed rail networks throughout Africa, linking the continent to facilitate industrialization, and the extensive construction of nuclear power plants throughout the African continent, to eliminate the power shortages that have been holding the continent back. Africa accounts for a sixth of the world's population, but generates only 4% of the electricity generated in the world.

South Africa's ANC: British Use Regime Change to Stop BRICS

by David Cherry and Ramasimong Phillip Tsokolibane

May 17—The ruling party in South Africa is now accusing the British government of plotting regime change. Meanwhile, some ruling party leaders are also declaring that the purpose of the ongoing regime change mobilization in South Africa, as also in Brazil, is to break up the BRICS.

Since July 25, 2014, the leader of LaRouche South Africa, Ramasimong Tsokolibane, has made clear that the British Empire, including its Wall Street satellite, is organizing regime change in South Africa and elsewhere, not only to destroy the BRICS and stop nuclear power development, but to depopulate Africa and much else, to obtain a world of perhaps a mere one billion people.

Zizi Kodwa, spokesman for the ruling African National Congress (ANC), told South Africa's *News24* on May 16 that the British Defense Ministry had been working to unseat President Zuma. He drew attention to a visit to South Africa in early June 2015, organized by the Royal College of Defence Studies (RCDS), ostensibly to "assess the political threats to continuing ANC rule in South Africa."

The British government had described the visit organized by the RCDS as part of a "global strategic studies" course for an international group of 18 military officers and civilian armed forces officials. Regime change organizing against the Zuma government was at fever pitch at the time of the visit, as it still is today.

According to Phil Miller, a British investigative reporter publishing on vice.com, the study group was officially tasked to "devise a medium term strategy, with concrete deliverables, for the party to retain power at the next general election." The report remains classified. The officers spent a good deal of time with enemies of the Zuma government. They "received a briefing at the Johannesburg Stock Exchange, and called in at HSBC [the British Empire bank formerly known as the Hongkong Shanghai Banking Corporation] for a working lunch." At Lonmin's offices, they "spent an afternoon with senior staff," according to Miller. Lonmin is the platinum mining company implicated in the 2012 orchestrated massacre of South African miners at Marikana that was used to damage the standing of the Zuma government.

Miller's article on vice.com, published earlier on May 16, was intended, however, to contribute to the *removal* of the Zuma government by taking the officers' visit at face value, and thus portraying the ANC as propped up by a former colonial power. But the ANC

agenciabrasil/Roberto Stuckert Filho

After the unconstitutional impeachment of Brazil President Dilma Rousseff, the ruling African National Congress party in South Africa charged that the British and the Obama Administration are using regime change to stop the BRICS. The five BRICS Heads of State are shown here at the 2014 G-20 summit in Brisbane, Australia, Nov. 15. From left: Russia: Vladimir Putin; India: Narendra Modi; Brazil: Rousseff; China: Xi Jinping; South Africa: Jacob Zuma.

shot back with the obvious. There are indications that there had been suspicions during the visit.

More broadly, ANC spokesman Kodwa "accused Britain and the United States of America of using undemocratic means to change a democratically elected government. 'It has done so in many other countries, working with America as part of a Western coalition, to unseat democratically elected government through undemocratic means. They [the British] are part of that agenda,' he said," according to *News24*.

Regime Change to Break the BRICS

The ANC is also now recognizing that regime change is designed to get South Africa out of the BRICS and crush BRICS. South African Water and Sanitation Minister Nomvula Mokonyane, who is also the ANC's national head of elections and campaigns, said so in addressing a memorial ceremony in Kwazulu-Natal reported April 30 by SABC, the state broadcaster.

Earlier, on April 13 in Gauteng province, the industrial heart of the country, a joint statement of the provincial ANC Women's League, ANC Youth League, and Mkhonto we Sizwe Military Veterans declared, according to Africa News Agency, that "calls for Zuma to

resign were influenced by the West, which was hell bent on targeting BRICS countries 'in pursuit of feeding their hunger for total control.' South Africa's opposition parties were also influenced by 'western powers,' they said." Youth League provincial chairman Matome Chiloane, in reading the statement, added that "The dirty hand of the West is fiddling in our country and using the opposition as their instruments to create chaos...." The joint statement was provoked by a very different declaration by the ANC Provincial Executive, which hinted that President Zuma should resign—reflecting the inroads of the regime changers into the ANC itself.

KwaZulu-Natal's provincial ANC leaders Super Zuma (no relation to the President) and Sihle Zikalala are also now attacking regime change as aimed against BRICS. Provincial ANC Chairman Zikalala, in a May 6 lecture at the University of Zululand covered by SABC, said that the formation of BRICS was a "game-changer for these major emerging economies from the cobweb of international money lending financial institutions," and for that reason, South Africa and Brazil were both under regime-change attack. The provinces of Gauteng and KwaZulu-Natal combined represent almost half of the population of South Africa.

www.ingramcontent.com/pod-product-compliance
Lightning Source LLC
Chambersburg PA
CBHW081159280526
45787CB00008B/3380